Our Guests

Cover Image by Charles Wysocki

HARVEST HOUSE PUBLISHERS

EUGENE, OREGON

Cover image: "Gingernut Valley" by Charles Wysocki

Wysocki Guest Book

Copyright © 2004 by Harvest House Publishers
Published by Harvest House Publishers
Eugene, Oregon 97402

ISBN 0-7369-1358-0

Cover art is copyrighted by Charles Wysocki and licensed by Mosaic Licensing, Walnut Creek, CA and may not be copied or reproduced without permission. For more information, please contact:

Mosaic Licensing
675 Ygnacio Valley Road, Suite B207
Walnut Creek, CA 94596
(925) 935-0889

Cover by Garborg Design Works, Minneapolis, Minnesota

Harvest House Publishers has made every effort to trace the ownership of all poems and quotes. In the event of a question arising from the use of a poem or quote, we regret any error made and will be pleased to make the necessary correction in future editions of this book.

Printed in Hong Kong

04 05 06 07 08 09 10 11 12 13 / NG / 10 9 8 7 6 5 4 3 2 1

Bless this house as we come and go.
Bless this house as the children grow.
Bless our families when they gather in.
Bless this house with love and friends.

AUTHOR UNKNOWN

Date   Guests

Date   Guests

Date   Guests

Date   Guests

Date　　　Guests

Date   Guests

Date   Guests

Date   Guests

Tap at our door! A welcome waits
As warm as are the logs aglow.
The buffetings of all the fates
We understand and know.

Come from the sunshine or the storm!
Come whether skies be gray or blue!
This hearth with sympathy is warm,
Our hearts have room for you.

EDGAR GUEST

Date   Guests

Date   Guests

Date   Guests

Date   Guests

Date   Guests

Date   Guests

Date   Guests

Date   Guests

Date   Guests

A house is built by human hands—
*B*ut a home is built by human hearts.

AUTHOR UNKNOWN

Date   Guests

Date   Guests

Date   Guests

Date   Guests

Date　　　Guests

Date   Guests

But every house where Love abides
And Friendship is a guest,
Is surely home, and home, sweet home;
For there the heart can rest.

HENRY VAN DYKE

Date   Guests

Date   Guests

Date   Guests

Date   Guests

Date   Guests

Date   Guests

Date   Guests

Date   Guests

Date   Guests

Be not forgetful to entertain strangers:
for thereby some have entertained angels unawares.

THE BOOK OF HEBREWS

Date   Guests

Date   Guests

Date   Guests

Date　　　Guests

Date   Guests

_____ _____

_____ _____

_____ _____

_____ _____

_____ _____

_____ _____

_____ _____

_____ _____

_____ _____

_____ _____

_____ _____

_____ _____

Date   Guests

Love begins at home,
and it is not how much we do...
but how much love we put in that action.

MOTHER THERESA

Date　　　Guests

Date   Guests

Date   Guests

Date   Guests

Date   Guests

Date   Guests

Date　　　Guests

Date   Guests

Date   Guests

A home is not a mere transient shelter:
its essence lies in the personalities of the people who live in it.

H.L. MENCKEN

Date   Guests

Date   Guests

Date   Guests

Date   Guests

Date   Guests

Date   Guests

Blest be the spot, where cheerful guests
retire to pause from toil,
and trim their ev'ning pair,
and every stranger finds a ready chair.

OLIVER GOLDSMITH

Date   Guests

Date   Guests

Date   Guests

Date   Guests

Date   Guests

Date   Guests

Date   Guests

Date   Guests

Date   Guests

Seek home for rest,
For home is best.

THOMAS TUSSER

Date   Guests

Date   Guests

Date   Guests

Date   Guests

Date   Guests

Date   Guests

God looks down well pleased to mark
In earth's dusk each rosy spark,
Lights of home and lights of love,
And the child the heart therof.

KATHERINE TYNAN

Date　　　Guests

Date   Guests

Date   Guests

Date   Guests

Date   Guests

Date   Guests

Date   Guests

Date   Guests

Date   Guests

Where thou art,
that is home.

EMILY DICKINSON

Date   Guests

Date   Guests

Date   Guests

Date   Guests

Date   Guests

Date   Guests

Date   Guests

Date   Guests

Date   Guests

Date   Guests

The little path that leads to home,
That is the road for me,
I know no finer path to roam,
With finer sights to see.

EDGAR GUEST